KT-512-596

Contents

1889-1918
Birth Of A Despot

EARLY YEARS

A photograph of Hitler as a one-year-old gives almost no clue to his future role in history as Europe's most despised dictator. He sits before the camera, a beautiful baby boy – sweet face topped with thick black hair, cut in a pudding basin style. His eyes, intense and penetrating, are particularly striking. Variously described by the people Hitler would meet as 'startling and unforgettable', or containing 'an indescribable flickering brightness', these eyes contributed greatly to Hitler's astounding ability to mould people – individuals, vast crowds, even an entire nation – to his own evil will.

▼ The infant Hitler stares innocently into the camera in 1890. His childhood was marred by a brutal father who treated him harshly.

HITLER'S PARENTS

Hitler inherited his eyes from his mother Klara, a striking, intense woman 23 years younger than her husband Alois. He was a brutal, domineering man, now on his third marriage. He worked as a customs official in the Austro-Hungarian Empire, a monarchy which ruled over most of eastern Europe. Adolf was born on 20 April 1889, in the small Austrian town of Braunau. The site of Hitler's birthplace has now been destroyed, to deter unwelcome pilgrimages from political fanatics who still see him as a great man.

The family moved to Linz, the capital of Upper Austria, and it was here that Hitler spent most of his childhood. By all accounts he hated his violent and ill-tempered father, but adored his mother. He carried a picture

This book is to be returned on or before
the last date stamped below.

0 4 FEB 2004

2 5 FEB 2004

1 6 MAR 2004

- 5 SEP 2013

22 NOV 2021

LIBRARY SCHOOL

Campus Library Services Limited

39326

WARWICK SCHOOL

Hitler

PAUL DOWSWELL

HODDER
Wayland

an imprint of Hodder Children's Books

© 2002 White-Thomson Publishing Ltd

Produced for Hodder Wayland by
White-Thomson Publishing Ltd
2/3 St Andrew's Place
Lewes
BN7 1UP

Other titles in this series:
Churchill
Kennedy
Stalin

Series concept: Alex Woolf
Editor: Philip de Ste. Croix
Design: Derek Lee
Consultant: Dr Corey Ross,
   University of Birmingham
Picture research: Shelley Noronha
   Glass Onion Pictures
Map artwork: Nick Hawken
Indexer: Amanda O'Neill

First published in Great Britain in 2002 by
Hodder Wayland, an imprint of Hodder
Children's Books

The right of Paul Dowswell to be identified as
the author has been asserted by him in
accordance with the Copyright, Designs and
Patents Act 1988.

All rights reserved. No part of this publication
may be reproduced, stored in a retrieval
system, or transmitted, in any form or by any
means without the prior written permission of
the publisher, nor be otherwise circulated in
any form of binding or cover other than that
in which it is published and without a similar
condition being imposed on the subsequent
purchaser.

British Library Cataloguing in Publication Data
Dowswell, Paul
   Adolf Hitler. – (20th century leaders)
   1. Hitler, Adolf, 1889-1945 2. Heads of state –
   Germany
   I. Title
   943'.086'092

ISBN 0 7502 3919 0

Printed in Hong Kong by Wing King Tong

Hodder Children's Books
A division of Hodder Headline Limited
338 Euston Road, London NW1 3BH

Picture acknowledgements: The publisher would
like to thank the following for permission to
use their pictures: AKG London 4, 5, 8, 12, 14
(bottom), 16, 20, 21, 22, 26, 27, 29, 35, 36, 38
(top), 45 (top), 46, 48, 51, 52, 53, 54 (Jewgeni
Chaldej), 57, 58; Associated Press (Hodder
Wayland Picture Library) 32; Imperial War
Museum, London (Hodder Wayland Picture
Library) 13, 17, 25, 31, 40 (top), 50, 60, 61;
Institute of Contemporary History and Wiener
Library 23, 28; Peter Newark's Historical
Pictures 14 (top); Peter Newark's Military
Pictures 30, 34, 40 (bottom), 41; Popperfoto 6,
7, 10, 18, 24, 33, 39, 42, 43, 47, 49, 55, 56, 59;
Staatsbibliothek Berlin (Hodder Wayland
Picture Library) 38 (bottom); Topham
Picturepoint 45 (bottom).

Cover picture: Imperial War Museum, London

of her with him for his entire life. When he came to power in Germany, he decreed that the date of his mother's death should become a day of honour for German mothers.

SCHOOL DAYS

Hitler was a bright child, but lazy, and he did not do well academically. Nonetheless he loved reading, especially books on war and soldiering. He was also very interested in art, and told his father he intended to become an artist or architect. Alois was horrified and replied 'Artist? No, never, as long as I live.'

His character seemed to have formed at an early age. One of his teachers, Dr Eduard Hümer, remembered him like this:

'He had definite talent, though in a narrow field. But he lacked self-discipline, being notoriously wilful, arrogant and bad-tempered. He reacted with ill-concealed hostility to advice or reproof; at the same time, he demanded of his fellow pupils their unqualified subservience, fancying himself in the role of leader.'

It was a very astute description, and one which many of Hitler's generals would recognize. It would seem especially apt in the closing years of the Second World War, when he led his armies into a series of military catastrophes which would result in the destruction of Germany.

▲ Hitler's adored mother, Klara, in a photographic portrait that clearly shows her intense gaze – a physical feature that her son inherited from her.

HERR SCHICKLGRUBER

Hitler's father was illegitimate, and for a while Alois was known by his mother's name Schicklgruber. He changed his name to Hitler in 1876, thirteen years before Adolf was born. Hitler's opponents, both in Germany and Britain and America, liked people to believe that the unattractive sounding 'Schicklgruber' was Hitler's real name, and used it to mock him in propaganda newsreel and radio broadcasts.

▲ Hitler at the age of 16. His wilful, arrogant personality is cleverly captured in this sketch by a fellow secondary school pupil.

EARLY DISAPPOINTMENTS

His father's death in 1903, when Hitler was 14, came as a relief to him. His mother was worried about Hitler's dream of becoming an artist, but she was more indulgent. When he left school at 16 with no formal qualifications, she paid for his attempts to win a place at the Vienna Academy of Fine Arts. But she died of cancer, aged only 48, and at 18 Hitler was left parentless. Still, he was able to use her small pension and savings to finance his fantasy of becoming an art student. But Hitler was rejected by both the Vienna Academy and the School of Architecture, events which led him into a period of deep depression.

EVIL INFLUENCES

In the years before the First World War, Hitler lived the life of a drifter. He painted views of Vienna and sold them as postcards to add to his small pension. He lived in hostels where he mingled with the city's down-and-outs. Almost penniless, he was forced to shovel snow to make enough money to eat. It was a difficult time, which Hitler would recall with the chilling words 'I owe it to that period that I grew hard'.

Vienna was a bustling city full of people from many countries, as well as citizens from the whole of the Austro-Hungarian Empire. During his stay in the city, influenced by Vienna's gutter press and political pamphlets then in circulation, Hitler developed the political convictions which would shape both his life and the fate of a continent. There grew in him a fierce hatred of the Jews and Slavs, a horror of the newly emerging political philosophy of communism, and a belief that those of Germanic stock were a superior 'master race'.

His anti-Semitism (hatred of Jews) was particularly intense. Hitler blamed Jews for everything that had gone wrong with his life, and for everything that he hated in the world. It was the Jews who, he said, had rejected him from the Vienna Academy; it was the Jews who had invented communism, which he despised.

WAR COMES TO EUROPE

Hitler moved to Munich in the south German region of Bavaria in 1913. He felt much more at home in a city which contained mostly Germans, rather than Vienna's mixture of Austrians, Czechs, Slavs, Jews and others. Then, in the summer of 1914, huge events swept over Europe. The assassination of the Austrian archduke Franz Ferdinand by a Serbian nationalist triggered a chain of events which dragged Germany and Austria-Hungary into war with most of the rest of Europe. With hindsight we now see the First World War as a dreadful disaster, but at the time many of Europe's young men greeted it as a marvellous opportunity to express their fierce, nationalistic pride. Hitler was no exception:

'I sank down upon my knees and thanked heaven out of the fullness of my heart for the favour of being permitted to live at such a time,' he wrote in *Mein Kampf*. He volunteered for the army and joined the 16th Bavarian Reserve Infantry Regiment.

▲ The Reichsratstrasse in Vienna, in the early twentieth century. During his time in Vienna Hitler developed political views that would ultimately leave the continent of Europe in ruins.

HITLER'S ANTI-SEMITISM

In this passage, from Hitler's book *Mein Kampf*, he describes his dawning 'realization' that Jews were the root of all human evil. It is typical of the type of obscene language that Nazis would later use to describe the Jewish people to the entire German nation.

'Was there any shady undertaking, any form of foulness...in which at least one Jew did not participate? On putting the probing knife carefully to that kind of abscess one immediately discovered, like a maggot in a putrescent [rotting] body, a little Jew who was often blinded by the sudden light.'

7

▲ Hitler, seated far right, with fellow soldiers of the 16th Bavarian Reserve Infantry Regiment. Despite the dangers that he faced in the trenches, Hitler enjoyed his time in the army greatly.

ARMY LIFE

Hitler spent the next four years serving with the army on the Western Front. Caught up in the fighting almost from the start of the war, at the First Battle of Ypres in France he saw his regiment cut down from 3,500 to 600 men in four days.

He served as a messenger, carrying orders by foot between company and regimental headquarters. While not actually in the trenches, Hitler constantly had to risk his life. He was twice awarded the Iron Cross for bravery, and was promoted to the rank of lance-corporal. As a boy he had been fascinated by war, and his experiences in battle did not disappoint him. The comradeship of his fellow soldiers, and the strict discipline of army life, confirmed his own beliefs in the glory of war. He looked back on this period with affection for the rest of his life.

GERMANY'S DEFEAT

Hitler was wounded twice – once in 1916 when he was shot through the leg, and again in October 1918 when he was gassed. He was recovering in hospital in November when he heard that Germany had surrendered. 'Everything went black before my eyes as I staggered back to my ward and buried my aching head between the blankets and pillow…I had not wept since the day I stood at my mother's grave, but now I could not help it,' he recalled.

News of Germany's defeat came as a great shock to Hitler, as it did to many German soldiers and civilians. The German army had defeated Russia in the east, and the war on the Western Front had recently seen great German victories. However, reversals following these victories had been kept secret from the German people, and now the German army was exhausted. Germany's leaders were also anxious to make peace because they feared a communist revolution at home, similar to the one that had swept through Russia in 1917.

A STAB IN THE BACK

All of this was ignored by many German soldiers who preferred to see their defeat as a grand betrayal by cowardly politicians who had 'stabbed them in the back'. In the terrible, bitter years after the war the entire German nation had to come to terms with the fact that two million fathers and sons had been killed for a lost cause. The idea that Germany had been betrayed was easy to accept because many people wanted to believe it.

Hitler both swallowed and fostered this myth, branding the politicians who had overseen the surrender as 'the November criminals'. Brooding and agonizing in his hospital bed, Hitler wrote that the days after the war 'were terrible to bear, and the nights still worse. During these nights my hatred increased, hatred for the originators of this dastardly crime.'

LOOKING FOR SCAPEGOATS

Hitler knew who to blame – the democratic politicians who had signed the armistice, and the communists who had brought Germany to the brink of revolution at the end of the war. But mostly he blamed the people he had come to hate in Vienna – the Jews. He began to see his life as a mission to avenge Germany's defeat and make her enemies pay. The loss of the war was a turning point. All too soon his hatred would find a suitable outlet.

HITLER AND THE WAR

'It created an extraordinary moral blunting in Hitler. He had friends who were killed every day...It created in him almost a desire to steep himself in the atmosphere of death. He had very clear links between that extraordinary environment and his willingness later on to embrace policies of annihilation.'

BRITISH HISTORIAN PROFESSOR RICHARD OVERY SPEAKING ABOUT THE INFLUENCE OF THE WAR ON HITLER'S CHARACTER

9

CHAPTER TWO

1918-1929
From Corporal To Party Leader

THE VERSAILLES TREATY

In Hitler's eyes, the loss of the war was followed by an equally terrible event – the Versailles Peace Treaty of 1919. Drawn up in an atmosphere of post-war bitterness this short-sighted, vengeful treaty imposed by the Allies* was designed to crush Germany once and for all. Germany had to accept responsibility for starting the war and was forced to pay 'reparations' (compensation) for war damage. Germany also had to give up territory both within its borders and all former overseas colonies, and limit its armed forces. The army was to be no bigger than 100,000 men, with no tanks or heavy artillery, and there was to be no air force or submarine fleet. Furthermore, no troops were to be stationed on the border with France.

Many Germans understandably regarded the treaty as an unforgivable humiliation – especially those who believed that they had not really lost the war. They pointed out that no enemy soldier had entered German territory by the time the war ended, and could not understand why their nation should have to accept such harsh terms. The treaty undermined the new post-war German government – the democratic Weimar Republic (so called because the new constitution was drawn up in

▼ Diplomats and politicians gather at the Versailles Peace Conference in 1919. Unfortunately for the world, most of the victorious countries were bent on taking revenge on Germany, rather than reconciliation.

* Principally Britain, France and the United States.

the German city of Weimar) – from the very beginnings of its fragile life. Hitler was to dedicate his life to destroying both the peace settlement and the Weimar Republic.

A NEW HOME

Corporal Hitler was not discharged from the army until 1920. In 1919 he was asked to work as an army political agent and spy on extremist political groups in Munich. His first mission was to infiltrate a small right-wing group called the German Workers' Party (GWP). They believed in a curious mixture of nationalist pride, crude anti-Semitism and economic ideas borrowed from the socialists. Hitler found their ideas so appealing that he joined them.

The GWP soon became an outlet for two exceptional, and hitherto unrealized, talents in Hitler. In the army he had not been promoted beyond lance-corporal because his officers thought he could not lead men. They had misjudged him. Hitler had an outstanding ability for organizing others. More importantly, the GWP discovered that he was a extraordinary speaker. Shortly after he joined, party leader Anton Drexler observed him addressing a meeting. 'Goodness,' Drexler said, 'He's got a gob on him. We could use him!'

BIRTH OF THE NAZI PARTY

In less than a year Hitler came to dominate the little party and in July 1921 he became its president. Crucially, he gave the party a distinctive voice and character. He introduced the swastika symbol and colourful banners. He transformed his hatred into a well-defined political agenda, offering Germany clear-cut scapegoats for their troubles – the communists and Jews – and a promise to restore German national pride. The party name was changed to

THE SWASTIKA 卐

One of the most recognizable political symbols of the twentieth century, the swastika was originally an ancient Asian good luck charm. Hitler borrowed it for his National Socialist party, and when he came to power the symbol became a national emblem for Germany.

Nationalsozialistische Deutsche Arbeiterpartei – National Socialist German Workers' Party – which soon became more commonly known in an abbreviated form as the Nazi Party. Hitler even introduced the ritual Nazi salute 'Heil' – a German word with many meanings; literally translated as 'Hail!' (Greetings!), it also evokes feelings of unity, salvation and well-being.

The party acquired a newspaper – the *Völkischer Beobachter* (People's Observer) – which would become a mouthpiece for the Nazis' extreme nationalist and anti-Semitic views. Hitler also established his own brutal private army under the leadership of a local army officer Captain Ernst Röhm. Known as the SA (*Sturmabteilung* – Storm Section) they both terrorized opponents and protected Hitler and fellow Nazis from the violence they provoked in political rivals. Many of these men were recruited from the ranks of embittered former soldiers who were unwilling to return to civilian life. Such men had banded together in groups known as the *Freikorps* (Free Corps).

▼ Hitler, centre, in Nuremberg, two months before the disastrous Beer Hall Putsch took place in Munich in 1923.

FERTILE GROUND

The combination of Nazi politics and Hitler's own personal magnetism as a political speaker was an irresistible mixture in the Munich of the early 1920s. After the shame of surrender and the Versailles Peace Treaty came further troubles for Germany. There was runaway inflation which wiped out the savings of the middle-classes. Then France humiliated Germany by occupying the Ruhr valley because of non-payment of war reparations. There was also mass unemployment. In Germany an atmosphere of lawlessness and contempt for the post-war government was in the air, and strikes and street fights between political opponents were common

In less than four years the Nazi party grew from a handful of oddballs to a major force in German politics with 56,000 members. Already the ranks of the party contained Nazis who would later become infamous throughout the world – men such as Alfred Rosenberg, Hermann Göring, Rudolf Hess and Julius Streicher.

▲ Mussolini, centre, with hands on hips, stands among fellow Italian fascists. At first, Hitler idolized the Italian dictator, but his friendship and political alliance with Mussolini would bring him a great deal of trouble.

ITALIAN ROLE MODEL

Hitler had been intrigued by the rise to power in Italy of Benito Mussolini – the leader of the Italian fascist party, who had seized power in 1922. Hitler hoped to follow his example. In November 1923, a group of Bavarian generals, government officials, and civil servants were attending a meeting in a large Munich beer hall. In an uprising that became known as the Beer Hall Putsch (coup), armed SA men burst in to the building and held them hostage. Then Hitler stood before them and announced that he was setting up a national government with the German war hero General Ludendorff, who had recently become a political ally. The hostages cheered wildly and Hitler, assured of their support, ordered their release.

MUSSOLINI AND ITALIAN FASCISM

Mussolini headed a political movement called the fascists. They were as intensely nationalistic and authoritarian as the Nazis, but largely lacking their anti-Semitic hatred. While Italy was gripped with strikes and lawlessness, the fascists had seized control of the country in a dramatic 'March on Rome' in 1922. Here thousands of Mussolini's supporters had headed for the Italian capital demanding power. Much to everyone's surprise, not least Mussolini's, the Italian king expressed support. He saw the fascists as a better alternative than a feared communist revolution, and within days Mussolini was prime minister.

Hitler gazes at the outside world during his stay in Landsberg prison in 1924.

THE PUTSCH FAILS

Next day Hitler and 2,000 Nazis marched to the Bavarian war ministry intending to seize control of the city. But the marchers were fired on by the police, and Hitler fled. In hiding he thought about committing suicide, but was talked out of it by Frau Hanfstängl, the wife of his press officer.

Arrested and tried for treason, Hitler declared 'There is no such thing as high treason against the traitors of 1918.' The court seemed to agree with him, and the sentence that he received was remarkably light. For trying to overthrow the government of Germany he was sent to Landsberg prison for less than a year.

TIME IN PRISON

Children playing with piles of worthless money in Germany in November 1923.

The putsch had failed, but it brought Hitler massive publicity. He was now a politician who was known throughout the country. Hitler used his time in prison well, dictating his political ideas to his secretary, Rudolf Hess, who had also been imprisoned in Landsberg following the failed putsch. These ideas were published in a book called *Mein Kampf* (*My Struggle*).

NAZI SUPPORT DECLINES

On his release, Hitler returned to politics with one vital lesson learned. Having failed to seize control through violence, he was now determined to come to power through legal means. This meant trying to use Germany's democratic process to his benefit. But for now he would have to wait. In the mid to late 1920s stability returned to

Germany as the currency was reformed, the burden of reparation payments was made easier and America provided economic aid. As the country prospered, Nazi support dwindled.

But over in the United States, a decade of prosperity that followed the First World War was about to turn into a spectacular slump. In 1929 the American Stock Market, and then the economy, collapsed. Economic aid to the nations of Europe dried up. In Germany banks failed, factories closed, and within a year four million people were out of work. For Hitler, a politician who fed on human hatred, misery on such a scale could only be good news.

MEIN KAMPF (MY STRUGGLE)

Originally titled *Four and a Half Years of Struggle against Lies, Stupidity, and Cowardice,* *Mein Kampf* is a dreary read. Yet Hitler's political manifesto became a sacred work that was regarded with religious awe by many Germans in the 1930s. Copies were given free to all newlyweds and often kept in special presentation boxes carved with Nazi symbols such as the swastika.

The book contains almost nothing original – being mainly a rehash of the political ideas Hitler picked up as a young man in Vienna. Yet *Mein Kampf* was also a chilling insight into Hitler's thoughts, intentions and methods. Nowhere in history is such a barbarous vision set out so clearly. Some of the main themes are:

• Hitler would lead the 'Aryan' race (people of pure Germanic blood) in a crusade to conquer and enslave the Slavs of eastern Europe and Russia, and provide *Lebensraum* (living space) for his people.

• The Soviet Union, and the communist regime that controlled it, was Germany's greatest enemy, and must be destroyed in a titanic struggle that would decide the fate of Europe for centuries to come.

• The Jews were the greatest enemy of mankind – the embodiment of evil. They were to be 'eradicated'.

Hitler's supporters were carried away by *Mein Kampf's* dreams of conquest and slavery, but they would better have dwelled on these words: 'Germany will either be a world power or not exist at all.' In the years to come Hitler would set out to fulfil that prophecy with brutal determination and terrible consequences.

CHAPTER THREE

1929-1934
The Road To Power

A POLITICAL ALLIANCE

In the period of unease and uncertainty that marked the new decade, Hitler made a clever alliance with another nationalist politician, Alfred Hugenberg. Like Hitler, Hugenberg was a racist, and he hated the Versailles Treaty as much as the Nazi leader did. Hugenberg also had something Hitler did not – a nationwide following for his Nationalist Party, control of national newspapers, and wealth and influence. A former director of the huge Krupp Steel company, Hugenberg knew some of the most powerful politicians, industrialists and businessmen in Germany.

Although many of these people found Hitler's views on Jews and other races too extreme, they were impressed by his opposition to communism. Such men began to make big donations to Nazi Party funds as they feared a repeat in their own countries of the 1917 Russian Revolution, when the old order was dramatically swept away by a bloody communist revolution. Both Hugenberg and the industrialists thought they could use Hitler to further their own ambitions and ends. But Hitler showed great skill in manipulating and using them instead.

NATIONWIDE PLATFORM

Hitler's Nazi Party now had the financial muscle to make its presence felt at a national level. Hitler's message, that Germany should rouse

▼ Nazi propaganda posters, such as this one by K. Stauber, liked to depict Hitler as a superhuman, heroic figure leading Germany out of her many troubles and on to victory.

HITLER THE PUBLIC SPEAKER

'As an orator Hitler had obvious faults. The timbre of his voice was harsh...He spoke at too great length; was often repetitive and verbose...(But) these shortcomings...mattered little beside the extraordinary impression of force, the immediacy of passion, the intensity of hatred, fury and menace conveyed by the sound of the voice...'

HISTORIAN ALAN BULLOCK, IN HIS BOOK
HITLER, A STUDY IN TYRANNY

'...one of the greatest speakers of the century...Adolf Hitler enters a hall. He sniffs the air. For a minute he gropes, feels his way, senses the atmosphere. Suddenly he bursts forth. His words go like an arrow to their target, he touches each private wound on the raw...'

NAZI PARTY MEMBER OTTO STRASSER, IN HIS BOOK *HITLER AND I*

itself and reassert its natural greatness, was skilfully conveyed in political posters. It struck home with great effectiveness – especially with the middle-class voters who had seen their cosy prosperity vanish. It also appealed to the more conservative working class, who faced unemployment and destitution.

Most effective of all though, was Hitler's own skill as a public speaker. The Nazis had become masters at staging political rallies, and at the heart of every important meeting was a speech by Hitler himself. Throughout the 1920s he had improved his natural abilities as a public speaker, a talent which he now used to great effect. Today, hearing him speak in newsreels in his harsh, guttural Austrian accent, he seems almost comical, but to German audiences in the 1930s his performances were hypnotically powerful.

MASS SUPPORT

With the country in deep economic depression, the Nazi Party made massive gains in the national elections of 1930. Over six million Germans voted for them, making the Nazis the second most powerful party in the country. Two years later Hitler felt strong enough to stand in the 1932 presidential elections against the 84-year-old German war hero General Paul von Hindenburg. Although he did not win, he took 37 per cent of the vote, after a campaign that saw the Nazi leader criss-cross the country by plane, speaking at twenty towns a week. In the pre-television era, such a gruelling schedule was essential. Wherever Hitler spoke, SA men would parade in the town and attack rival political meetings.

His popularity with the general public prompted some leading German politicians to befriend him – despite his extreme policies and the obvious brutality of his party.

▲ Hitler, with the German president Paul von Hindenburg. Both men disliked each other, but saw the advantage for themselves in working together.

GERMANY'S POLITICAL SYSTEM IN 1933

REICHSTAG: The German parliament, based in Berlin, containing elected political representatives, known as deputies, from all over the country.

THE CABINET: The group of ruling politicians known as ministers – each in charge of a particular area or department of the German government.

CHANCELLOR: The chief minister – an office similar to prime minister.

PRESIDENT: The head of state – an office similar to that of monarch, only it was an elected position rather than an hereditary one.

NAZI SEATS IN THE REICHSTAG BETWEEN 1928 AND 1933

1928	1930	July 1932	1933
12 seats	107 seats	230 seats	288 seats
Others 479	Others 470	Others 378	Others 359

They hoped that an alliance with the Nazis would enable them to seize or hold on to power themselves.

As unemployment rose to six million, the Nazis secured 230 out of 608 seats in the German Reichstag (parliament). Still a long way from an overall majority, they were, nonetheless, the largest political party. This made Hitler the most powerful politician in Germany.

INTO OFFICE

Another election late in 1932 gave the Nazis 196 seats. Their support seemed to be dwindling. Despite this, they were still the largest party, and Germany's political leaders knew they needed Hitler's co-operation to rule effectively. Chancellor Franz von Papen and President Hindenburg decided to bring Hitler into the government, and offered him the post of vice-chancellor. Hitler turned them down, demanding the chancellorship. There followed months of political deadlock, and Hitler cleverly bided his time. Finally, fearing the country was on the brink of civil war, President Hindenburg gave in to Hitler's demand. In January 1933 the Nazi leader became chancellor of Germany.

Hindenburg and von Papen were sympathetic to many of Hitler's policies, and thought they could control his more extreme measures. A deal was agreed whereby the Nazis were only allowed three members in the cabinet, and von Papen would remain as vice-chancellor.

But once Hitler was given his chance, there was no stopping him. One of his closest allies, Hermann Göring, was given the job of minister of the interior. He immediately replaced hundreds of civil servants with Nazi officials, and reorganized the Prussian political police into a Nazi-controlled secret police known as the Gestapo.

SEIZING TOTAL POWER

Still without a majority in the Reichstag (which meant political opponents could block new Nazi policies by uniting to vote against them) Hitler persuaded President Hindenburg to call another election. Before the election could be held, the Reichstag was burned to the ground on the night of 27 February 1933. Hitler declared that the fire was a signal for a communist revolution, and demanded to be granted emergency powers at this time of national crisis. Civil rights were suspended and 4,000 communist opponents were arrested.

The election called before the fire was held in March. Despite their control of the police and the army, and the violent oppression of political opponents, the Nazis only managed to gain 288 seats (43.9 per cent of the vote) – still short of a majority. A final act of political intimidation was needed to ensure Hitler the absolute power he wanted.

HERMANN GÖRING

A fighter pilot during the First World War, Göring joined Hitler's party in 1922. His upper-class background helped the Nazis appeal to middle-class voters. He became commander of the German air force and Hitler's deputy. A stout, luxury-loving man, he turned into a drug addict and became a figure of fun to many Germans. He fell from favour with Hitler during the war, and committed suicide after he was sentenced at the post-war Nuremberg Trials to hang for his war crimes.

THE NIGHT OF THE LONG KNIVES

After Hitler seized power in Germany there was still one area of opposition to his absolute rule, and it was inside his own party. Since the foundation of the party, Ernst Röhm's SA had grown from a small band of street-brawling thugs into a formidable force of some two million men.

But now Röhm was an embarrassment – ill-mannered and outspoken, he was keen to take over the army and push through some of the Nazis more radical policies, such as depriving German industrialists of their wealth and power. Hitler, on the other hand, saw the support of both the regular army and Germany's industrialists as essential to his plans for future conquest. As the SA had grown, Hitler had formed his own personal bodyguard, the SS (*Schutzstaffel* – Protection Squad). On the night of 29/30 June 1934, the SS arrested and executed Röhm, and around 400 other rivals and opponents within the Nazi Party. The massacre became known as 'The Night of the Long Knives'.

Following the fire, the Reichstag deputies met in the Potsdam Garrison church just outside Berlin. Here, surrounded by thuggish SA men, Hitler demanded that the deputies should grant him dictatorial powers for four years in a bill known as the Enabling Act. Outside the building further ranks of SA men and other Nazis chanted 'We want the bill – or fire and murder.' In this terrifying atmosphere the Enabling Act was passed by a huge majority – 441 votes to 94. When President Hindenburg died in August 1934 Hitler announced he would merge the office of chancellor and president into one, under the title *Führer* (Leader). Germans were asked to vote on this issue, and 89.9 per cent of those who did so supported it. Hitler was now the unquestioned absolute ruler of Germany.

▲ On the day of the Reichstag elections in March 1933, members of the SS (right of picture) were deployed on the streets alongside the regular police to keep order. The SS were later responsible for carrying out Hitler's 'Night of the Long Knives'.

CHAPTER FOUR

1933-1939
Life In Nazi Germany

'FANTASTIC HOOLIGANS'

With Hitler's hold on power secure, he now began to put into effect the cruel fantasy he had depicted in *Mein Kampf*. The British Ambassador in Berlin, Sir Horace Rumbold, watched in astonishment and reported 'Many of us…have a feeling that we are living in a country where fantastic hooligans and eccentrics have got the upper hand.' To outsiders, and Germans who did not support Hitler, it really did seem as if the lunatics had taken over the asylum.

Not everything the Nazis did was mad or bad. The Government tackled the unemployment problem with great success by ordering huge public works such as the building of Germany's *Autobahn* (motorway) system. Yet even this had a military motive, enabling the German army to move more quickly around the country.

In the years before the Second World War the Nazis infiltrated German society to the extent that almost every aspect of daily life was controlled by the Party. Presiding over these extraordinary changes were Dr Joseph Goebbels, Hitler's gifted propaganda minister, and Heinrich Himmler, his mild-mannered but remarkably callous chief of police.

▼ Hitler's propaganda minister, Joseph Goebbels, studies a newspaper. Every aspect of the German media, from cinema to the press, was closely controlled by the Nazi Party.

THE NAZIS AND THE MEDIA

Taking up Hitler's ideas, Goebbels spread the Nazi message via newspapers, radio broadcasts, newsreel (cinema news), and carefully staged rallies and pageants. No one in history had ever used the media so effectively to further their own political ends.

There was total censorship of any criticism of the Nazi regime, or any news unfavourable to its image. Goebbels, under Hitler's direction, also decreed that every form of entertainment should contain a political message glorifying the Nazis or condemning their enemies. Newspapers such as the *Völkischer Beobachter* (People's Observer) and *Der Stürmer* (The Stormtrooper) constantly hammered home the message of the need for conquest, and the destruction of communism and the Jews. Books deemed undesirable were destroyed, often in dramatic, night-time bonfires. One author whose books were burned recalled the words of nineteenth-century German poet Heinrich Heine: 'Whenever books will be burned, men also, in the end, are burned.'

▼ Rallies such as this were an opportunity to impress the citizens of Germany, and the rest of the world, with a display of Nazi power and unity.

FROM WORM TO DRAGON

Huge rallies were held, especially on important occasions in the Nazi calendar such as the anniversary of their seizure of power in 1933. The most famous of these were the Nuremberg Rallies. Here Hitler was greeted by a crowd around half a million strong, with a hysteria nowadays reserved for pop stars. Throughout the country millions of Germans would take part in parades that amazed everyone with their impression of order and strength. Goebbels commented 'At such meetings the individual changes from a little worm into part of a large dragon.'

HITLER AS GOD

Nazi propaganda often presented Hitler as a god-like leader.

'Führer, my Führer, sent to me from God, protect and maintain me throughout my life. Thou who hast saved Germany from deepest need, I thank thee today for my daily bread. Remain at my side and never leave me, Führer, my Führer, my faith, my light. Heil my Führer!'

GRACE BEFORE MEALS, TAUGHT TO GERMAN CHILDREN DURING THE NAZI ERA

ENFORCING NAZI RULE

Those not taken in by the persuasive propaganda of Dr Goebbels had Himmler and his secret police – the Gestapo – to convince them to toe the line. In office Hitler dealt with opponents with the same brutality his SA had shown in the street fighting of the 1920s – only on a much larger scale. Enemies were carted off to German concentration camps such as Dachau to be beaten, starved and worked to death. The Nazis created an oppressive, stifling society in which neighbour was invited to spy on neighbour, colleague on colleague, and even children were encouraged to report their own parents if they overheard them criticizing Hitler or the Nazi party.

Children sometimes betrayed their parents without meaning to. In 1934, for example, a Nazi teacher in Berlin

▼ Like an emperor, Hitler surveys the adoring crowd at a Nazi rally.

was teaching his class anti-Semitic propaganda. One child stood up and said 'My daddy says Jews are not damnably vile.' The father was immediately arrested and beaten up.

YOUTH MOVEMENTS

Hitler was especially concerned that the youth of Germany should grow up to be good Nazis. They should, in the party's words, 'be educated physically, mentally and morally in the spirit of National Socialism.' In 1936 a law proclaimed 'The future of the German people depends on its youth. The entire German youth must therefore be prepared for its future duties.' In effect, this meant that all German boys were to be trained as soldiers and all German girls were to ready themselves for their greatest role in life – motherhood.

▲ Hitler's chief of police, Heinrich Himmler, was responsible for organizing some of the Nazis' worst atrocities.

Two organizations were set up to indoctrinate German children – the Hitler Youth for boys, and the League of German Maidens for girls. Political indoctrination was not just confined to the youth groups. School books all echoed the Nazi message that Germany should become strong, and that communism and the Jews were the world's greatest evils. For example, children's fairy tales were rewritten with the Jews replacing witches and wolves as nasty, evil figures. Even the questions in mathematics text books took on a warlike aspect, as boys were asked to work out bombers' fuel capacities or artillery shell trajectories in preparation for their future roles as airmen or soldiers.

THE JEWS

Now that they controlled Germany, the Nazis turned their violent hatred of the Jews into government policy. Jewish academics, lawyers and civil servants were dismissed from their jobs. A nationwide boycott of Jewish businesses and shops was declared in 1933, and the 'Nuremberg Laws' of

GERMAN YOUTH

'I resented seeing such a small child in the dignified uniform, but like most children he loved the military effects and his report soon listed such accomplishments as being able to march, make maps, find directions and shoot, and under the heading of "Party accomplishment" were listed "Fervour for Nazi teaching", "Knowledge of Hitler songs", and "Knowledge of Hitler's biography".'

GERMAN MOTHER, RECALLING HER SON'S EXPERIENCES IN THE HITLER YOUTH

'The League of German Maidens kept us busy. Often we had no time for homework. We were lectured a lot on National Socialist ideology and most of it went over our heads. We were told from an early age to prepare for motherhood and in the eyes of our beloved leader, the mother was the most important person in the nation.'

GERMAN GIRL, RECALLING HER TIME IN THE LEAGUE OF GERMAN MAIDENS

▼ Hitler greets adoring members of the League of German Maidens. The Nazi leader was aware of his attraction to women, and cleverly exploited it to gain and hold on to political power.

B.d.M. begrüßt den FÜHRER

1935 deprived Jews of German citizenship and forbade marriage between Jew and 'Aryan' (this was a term used by the Nazis to mean a person belonging to the German race). Jewish children were excluded from state schools, and Jews were banned from parks, sports stadiums and swimming pools. Jews were often attacked in the street, or had the windows of their homes smashed.

▲ With their long beards and distinctive headgear, traditional Jews were all too easy to spot in the street, and were regularly bullied by Nazi soldiers and citizens alike.

On the night of 9/10 November 1938, the Jewish community was attacked mercilessly on an occasion known as Crystal Night (a reference to the shattered splinters of glass windows). 7,500 shops and 400 synagogues were looted and then destroyed, and 20,000 Jews were rounded up and imprisoned.

Between 1933-1939 half of all Jews in Germany left the country, including

CRYSTAL NIGHT

'Berlin's man in the street, at long last, had the opportunity of filling himself out again. Fur coats, carpets, valuable textiles, were all to be had for nothing. The people were enraptured.'

JOSEPH GOEBBELS, WRITING IN HIS DIARY ABOUT CRYSTAL NIGHT

NAZI SLOGANS

'Strength Through Joy'

'Children, Church and Kitchen' (for women)

'One People, One Nation, One Leader'

'The Jews Are Our Misfortune'

'Our Last Hope – HITLER'

'Guns Before Butter'

many famous and gifted citizens, such as the scientist Albert Einstein. Those who stayed either expected things to get better, or were simply unable to afford to leave or find countries willing to accept them. When war came in 1939, their treatment would get unimaginably worse.

USELESS EATERS

The Jews were not the only group to suffer the cruelty of the Nazis. Slavs, gypsies, negroes – all were considered *Untermensch* (subhuman) and treated with contempt. There was also a heartless disregard for the weak, sometimes referred to as 'useless eaters' in characteristically brutal Nazi language. Those with physical and mental handicaps were sterilized. After the war broke out they were murdered.

▼ In this illustration from a Nazi school book, 'Aryan' children drive Jewish children and a Jewish teacher from their school. Books such as this corrupted the minds of German boys and girls.

HITLER'S PRIVATE LIFE

'A woman must be a cute, cuddly naïve little thing – tender, sweet and stupid.'

HITLER, ON HIS IDEAL FEMALE

With only the evidence of photographs and newsreel, the adulation Hitler inspired is a puzzle to us now. Memorably described by one biographer, Robert G. L. Waite, as looking like 'an apprentice waiter in a second-class Viennese café', the German leader had a host of unappealing personal characteristics. Most notably, he had a very childish personality. Although he could be extremely charming and pleasant, he regularly behaved like a spoiled, sulking child, or exploded into childlike rages. He constantly sucked on sweets or ate chocolate. He engaged in staring games with dinner guests, and rarely laughed, except at other people's misfortunes.

He was a vegetarian who adored his pet German Shepherd dog, and had an uncommon care for the welfare of animals, which contrasted oddly with his disregard for human suffering.

Hitler liked to have beautiful women in his company, although he hated it if any had their own strong opinions, or dared to argue or disagree with him. His love life has been the subject of much speculation. He fell in love with his niece Geli Raubal and although most historians agree that they did not have a physical relationship, he was insanely jealous of her, and forbade her to have boyfriends. Hitler's behaviour drove her to suicide.

His most famous relationship was with Eva Braun, his photographer's assistant. Eva (seen with Hitler above right) was 17 when she first met him, twenty-three years his junior. She remained Hitler's loyal and secret companion through all his years in power. They married the day before their joint suicide at the end of the war. Her diary, which survived the war, is a sad little document, full of complaints about the way Hitler treated her. His armament minister Albert Speer reported a conversation they had when Hitler declared in front of her: 'A highly intelligent man should take a primitive and stupid woman…Lots of women are attracted to me because I am unmarried…It's the same as with a movie actor. When he marries he loses a certain something for the women who adore him.'

CHAPTER FIVE

1935-1939
The Road To War

DREAMS OF CONQUEST

Hitler had made no secret of his plans for conquest. Poland, the farmlands of Ukraine, the vast plains and oilfields of Russia – all were to be conquered, their peoples displaced, enslaved or killed to make *Lebensraum* (living space) for the German race. Everything he intended to do to Germany's eastern neighbours was laid out for all to see in *Mein Kampf*.

But before the Nazis could start on their conquests there were practical matters to sort out. Germany must rearm and German people outside the German border must be brought into the 'Reich' (empire). Allies too should be sought. Hitler saw Fascist Italy as a natural friend, and hoped that Britain too would side with him.

▼ The launch of the battlecruiser *Admiral Scheer* becomes an excuse for a display of Nazi power. Hitler was determined to make Germany the strongest military nation in Europe.

TEARING UP VERSAILLES

The Treaty of Versailles expressly forbade Germany from building up its military strength. So Hitler set about persuading his fellow Europeans that Germany was not a threat to them, and that a strong Germany would be an invaluable defence against the Soviet Union. Everything was done slowly and carefully – one move at a time – so as not to startle his neighbours into aggressive opposition.

Germany had lost the Saar territory on its western border to France after the First World War. In 1935 a plebiscite (referendum) there returned the region to Germany. Later that year he negotiated a navy treaty in which Britain recognized Germany's right to rearm. Conscription (compulsory military service) was introduced too. In 1936 Hitler sent troops into the 'demilitarized' Rhineland on the French border – an act totally forbidden by the Versailles Treaty. Britain and France protested, but neither were willing to back up their protest with force. Also in that year Hitler made alliances with Mussolini's Italy, and Japan. Meanwhile Germany began to build up its military strength with a vengeance – at first secretly, and then openly. Between 1936 and 1939 spending on arms went up 600 per cent.

THE THIRD REICH

The Nazis referred to their regime as the Third Reich – a German word broadly meaning kingdom or empire. The First Reich was the Holy Roman Empire of the Middle Ages. The Second Reich was a period between 1871-1918 when Germany was ruled by the kings of Prussia.

▼ In an act expressly forbidden by the Versailles Treaty, the German army marches into the 'demilitarized' Rhineland in 1936.

PREPARING FOR WAR

'Every publicly supported policy for creating employment must be judged by one criterion alone: is it or is it not needed for the restoration of the German nation's fighting capability?'

HITLER TO GOVERNMENT MINISTERS, 1933

▲ Hitler watches a Nazi military parade in the Austrian capital, Vienna, shortly after the German occupation of Austria in March 1938.

BOLDER MOVES

Everything had gone better than Hitler had dared to imagine. Britain and France especially seemed unwilling to stop him. In these countries there was some sympathy for Hitler. Many people admired the Nazis' anti-Communist stance. Also, by the 1930s, there was considerable support for the view that the Versailles Treaty had been too harsh on Germany.

Hitler decided to push his luck. In March 1938, after a tense month when Hitler and other Nazi leaders had threatened the Austrian Government with invasion, German troops marched into Hitler's former homeland. Again, Britain and France did nothing, and the jubilant reception he received from the Austrian people gave Hitler and the world no doubt that this was a popular move. In April 1938 a plebiscite was held throughout the Reich and 99.75 per cent of Austrians voted for their country to be united with Germany.

THE CZECHOSLOVAKIAN CRISIS

With Austria in German hands, much of the west of Czechoslovakia was now surrounded by German territory. The Czechoslovakian border region of Sudetenland contained some three million German-speakers, many of whom were supporters of the Nazis. Using this as an excuse, Hitler planned to seize the country by plotting with the leaders of the Sudeten Germans, who began to demand their independence. As relations between the Czechs and Germans deteriorated, the Czech leader Eduard Benes turned to France and Britain for help.

CHAMBERLAIN THE APPEASER

British prime minister Neville Chamberlain immediately flew to Germany to meet Hitler and try to settle the crisis. Chamberlain championed a policy known as 'appeasement'. The basis of this policy was that it recognized that Germany had been badly treated at the end of the First World War, and that it was right for the British to make concessions, to heal the mistrust and ill feeling between Britain and Germany.

Nowadays, appeasement is seen as a cowardly reaction to Nazi bullying, but at the time Chamberlain's policy was widely popular. After all, the dreadful slaughter of the First World War was a recent memory in Britain, and people did not want to go to war again.

However, despite Chamberlain's appeasement policy, Hitler's threats to invade Czechoslovakia could not be ignored. Britain and France declared they would defend the Czechs, and prepared for war. But both nations were extremely uneasy about this. As Chamberlain famously said in a broadcast at the time: 'How horrible, fantastic, incredible it is, that we should be digging trenches and trying on gas masks here because of a quarrel in a faraway country between peoples of whom we know nothing.'

▼ The British prime minister Neville Chamberlain arrives in Munich to meet Hitler in September 1938. The Nazi leader cleverly exploited Chamberlain's desperate desire to keep the peace in Europe.

Hitler's approach could not be more different. In a speech in Berlin, broadcast to the German people, he said: 'I believe that the time has come when one must mince matters no longer...For in the last resort Herr Benes has seven million Czechs, but here (in Germany) there stands a people of over seventy-five millions.' Benes, Hitler demanded, must hand over the Sudetenland. He went on 'My patience is at an end...The decision now lies in his hands: peace or war.'

▲ British cartoonist David Low's famous sketch drawn in response to the Nazi-Soviet Pact. It shows Hitler and Stalin greeting one another over the dead body of a Polish soldier.

PEACE IN OUR TIME?

Chamberlain flew back to Germany, determined to salvage a compromise. In a meeting with Hitler and French and Italian representatives, but not the Czechs, it was agreed that the Sudetenland should be handed over to Germany. Chamberlain returned to England and declared 'I believe it is peace in our time.'

But he had totally misjudged the German dictator. Six months later the new Czech president, an ageing judge named Emil Hacha, was summoned to Berlin. Hitler threatened his country with dire consequences if he did not agree to a German occupation. In March 1939, German troops marched unopposed into Prague.

POLAND AND THE SOVIET UNION

Continuing with his plans to expand eastward, Hitler now turned his attention to Poland, making a series of unreasonable demands for Polish territory. Britain and France, humiliated by Hitler's undermining of the agreement they had reached at Munich, and determined to stop Germany becoming too powerful a nation in Europe, now offered an alliance with the Poles. Throughout the summer of 1939, all four nations prepared for war.

In Germany that summer Hitler and his foreign minister Joachim von Ribbentrop pulled off an amazing diplomatic alliance with their arch enemies the Soviet Union. Unlikely as the alliance seemed, it suited both countries very well. Hitler did not want to have to fight the French and British

THE NAZI-SOVIET PACT

'Everything I undertake is directed against Russia. If the West is too stupid or too blind to understand this, then I will be forced to reach an understanding with the Russians, smash the West, and then turn all my concentrated strength on the Soviet Union.'

HITLER'S SECRET THOUGHTS ON THE
NAZI-SOVIET PACT

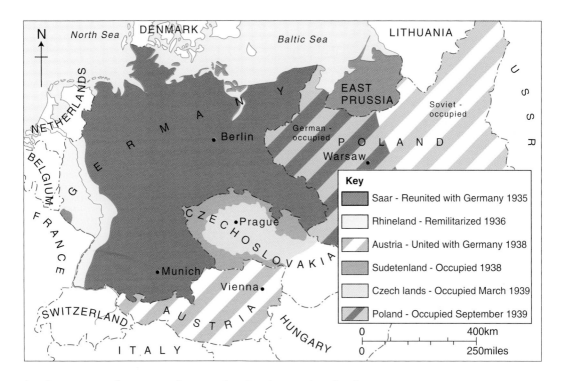

Key

■	Saar - Reunited with Germany 1935
□	Rhineland - Remilitarized 1936
▨	Austria - United with Germany 1938
■	Sudetenland - Occupied 1938
▨	Czech lands - Occupied March 1939
▨	Poland - Occupied September 1939

0   400km
0   250miles

in the west at the same time as the Soviet Union in the east. Stalin, in turn, wanted to buy time. The Soviet Union was well aware of Hitler's ambitions in the east, but its army was weak and disorganized. Ribbentrop and the Soviet foreign minister Molotov signed the so called Nazi-Soviet Pact on 23 August 1939. Each promised not to attack the other, and also secretly agreed to divide Poland, and other territories, between them.

WAR BEGINS

The fate of Poland was sealed. On 1 September 1939 German tanks and troops rolled over the border, and German bombers attacked the capital Warsaw. Hitler was still unsure if the French and British would call his bluff. 'They are little worms,' he sneered. But this time the worm turned, and by 3 September Britain and France had declared war on Germany.

▼ German troops overturning Polish border markers as they advance into the country in September 1939.

35

CHAPTER SIX

1939-1941
The Years Of Victory

GERMANY ADVANCES

Hitler began the Second World War full of swaggering confidence. 'I am now fifty and at the height of my powers. It is better war should come now rather than in five years time when Mussolini and I will be older,' he said.

▼ The German tactic of *Blitzkrieg*, developed by generals such as Heinz Guderian (below right), contributed to the speed of the German army's advance across Europe and Russia.

His confidence was entirely justifiable. For the next two years the military might of Nazi Germany would shock the world with such triumphs that Hitler began to believe that he could do no wrong.

The years of preparation for war paid off. Germany's army, full of young soldiers fresh from Nazi indoctrination in the Hitler Youth, was the best in Europe. The Polish campaign was also the first time the new tactic of *Blitzkrieg*

BLITZKRIEG

Hitler's early victories were won using a new tactic known as *Blitzkrieg*. Fast-moving tanks, self-propelled artillery and motorized infantry, supported by dive-bombers and fighter aircraft, were launched against often larger armies.

Developed by far-sighted generals such as the brilliant Heinz Guderian, *Blitzkrieg* was designed to keep battles mobile, and prevent the stalemate that was typical of the trench warfare of the First World War. It worked well – Germany conquered most of Europe with minor casualties and minimum use of resources.

(lightning war) was put to the test, and the results were incredibly successful. Within days, western Poland had been overrun. When Soviet troops invaded from the east to occupy territory up to the River Bug, the fate of Poland was sealed. During the Second World War no other country would lose such a large percentage of its population. As well as having many of its cities destroyed, Poland lost nearly one in five (17.5 per cent) of its population.

Behind the tanks and soldiers came Heinrich Himmler's SS *Einsatzgruppen* (special forces) – troops given the grisly task of carrying out the Nazi policies of racial resettlement and persecution. The Poles were the first people to discover first hand what Hitler's racial policies entailed. Anyone considered capable of organizing resistance to the Nazi invaders – from army officers to teachers and academics – was killed, and Poland's Jews were rounded up and confined in ghettos. Many were later exterminated. During the period of Nazi occupation nearly three million Polish Jews were murdered.

RACE WAR

Hitler issued these orders to his generals on the eve of the German invasion of Poland.

'Close your hearts to pity. Act brutally. 80 million people must obtain what is their right...The wholesale destruction of Poland is the objective. Speed is the chief thing. Pursuit until complete annihilation. Whatever we find in the shape of an upper class in Poland is to be liquidated...The increased severity of the racial struggle permits of no legal restriction; the methods used...will ensure that the Polish intelligentsia cannot throw up a new leader class.'

MORE VICTORIES

Hitler's success in Poland did not, as he had hoped, lead to any kind of peace settlement with his enemies in the west. Hitler and his generals were especially reluctant to fight against Britain, a country which they considered as a natural ally. Hitler admired the British Empire, and he felt that the British and Germans shared the same racial origins. However, he realized that before the Soviet Union could be conquered, Germany had to ensure its western flank was secure.

▲ Motorized German
troops drive past German
army signposts set up to
direct them during the
invasion of Denmark in
April 1940.

▼ German soldiers
march through the streets
of Paris on 14 June 1940.
France surrendered
shortly afterwards.

In April 1940 Denmark and Norway were occupied in another lightning campaign. In May the Germans launched an offensive against France. In the First World War the German army spent four years and suffered 1.8 million casualties failing to overrun France. Now Hitler and his generals did it in six weeks. And they lost only 27,000 men in the process.

By the end of June the Nazi leader had achieved his greatest victory. In 1918 representatives of Germany's defeated government were brought to the forest of Compiègne in France to sign the armistice accepting defeat. Now French leaders were brought to the same spot to undertake the same duty. The railway car where the 1918 ceremony took place was even bought from a Paris Museum for the occasion. Newsreels of the event show Hitler in a state of childish glee. He was so delighted he even danced a little jig for the camera. The day after, he went sightseeing in Paris and visited Napoleon's tomb. The victory against France inspired new levels of confidence in him. 'I shall go down in history as the greatest German of them all,' he told his entourage.

THE BATTLE OF BRITAIN

Then, Hitler turned his attention to Britain. His strategy, encouraged by Air Marshal Göring, head of Germany's *Luftwaffe* (air force), was to win control of the sky and then mount a seaborne invasion across the English Channel. But this was to be Hitler's first defeat. The Battle of Britain, as it became known, began in August 1940. German bomber and fighter planes droned across the Channel from bases in France and were met with fierce resistance. In a campaign which has since become legendary, around 1,500 Royal Air Force pilots took on the German air force. Many were from the British Commonwealth, or Poles and Czechs who had escaped from their conquered nations. Almost one in three were killed in the campaign. But so many *Luftwaffe* planes were lost, Hitler abandoned his invasion plans, and settled instead for a night-time bombing campaign. Destructive it may have been, but as the British and Americans found out later in the war, bombing alone would never defeat an enemy. Besides, in Hitler's mind there were more important tasks to attend to.

▼ Royal Air Force pilots rush to their fighter aircraft during the Battle of Britain. The defeat of the German *Luftwaffe* was Hitler's first serious reversal.

HITLER AND ITALY

> '*My unshakeable friendship for Italy and the Duce (Mussolini) may well be held to be an error on my part. It is in fact quite obvious that our Italian alliance has been of more service to our enemies than to ourselves.*'
>
> HITLER, REVIEWING HIS ALLIANCE WITH MUSSOLINI

▲ Hitler's alliance with Mussolini (left in picture) actually hindered Germany's cause during the war.

▼ Hitler with Nazi generals Jodl and Keitel. As the war went on, Hitler took less and less notice of the advice of his senior commanders.

ITALY INTERVENES

Hitler as a man had so many appalling characteristics it is easy to overlook any positive aspects in his personality, but loyalty was one of them. Mussolini had supported him before the war, and Hitler, in turn, would support the Italian dictator to the end – often at great cost to Germany.

As the German armies swept through Europe, Mussolini had watched with admiration and some envy. Nevertheless he kept Italy out of the war until he was totally convinced that the Germans had the upper hand. Then, declaring he had an 'appointment with history', he committed his nation to war. Italian armies advanced on several fronts against French and British troops, with limited success. They also attacked Greece quite disastrously. The failure of the campaign there brought Germany into the war in south-east Europe. Hitler's armies won more brilliant victories in Yugoslavia, Crete and Greece.

OPERATION BARBAROSSA

The campaign in south-east Europe was an unwanted distraction from Hitler's main interest – the invasion of the Soviet Union. Hitler was so determined to carry out this next grand stage in his plan, codenamed Operation Barbarossa, that he followed it through although there were still

★

A German soldier pauses by a burning house in the early stages of Operation Barbarossa – the invasion of the Soviet Union.

unresolved problems on other fronts. Britain was undefeated, and still had forces in north Africa which the Germans had to oppose. Troops earmarked for the Soviet invasion had been tied up in the Balkans. Germany was wasting time and effort supporting her ally Italy. Yet still Hitler proceeded.

THE INVASION BEGINS

As dive bombers swooped overhead, 3,500 German tanks and other armoured vehicles and three million troops crossed over the German/Soviet border at 3.15 a.m. on 22 June 1941. It was the most momentous invasion in history. Hitler expected the campaign to take two months. He was so confident of success that no plans were made to equip the German army with winter clothing or equipment.

German troops swept forward so swiftly that their supply lines struggled to keep up with them. As convoys carrying fuel, food and munitions sped down the dusty roads of the Russian plain chasing the advancing soldiers, they passed huge columns of bedraggled Soviet prisoners of war.

By the autumn of 1941 advanced units of the German army were so close to Moscow that they could see sunlight glinting on the Kremlin's golden domes. All that lay between Hitler's dream of a German empire in the east were the remains of the Soviet army and the first falls of snow that marked the beginning of the Russian winter.

WARWICK LIBRARY SCHOOL

CHAPTER SEVEN

1941-1944
The Tide Turns

MISSED OPPORTUNITIES

In the first heady months of the campaign, it would have been difficult to believe that the invasion of the Soviet Union would be Hitler's greatest mistake, and one that would have huge consequences for Germany, and Europe.

For twenty years before the invasion, the peoples of the Soviet Union had been ruled by a communist regime whose cruelty and ruthlessness often matched that of the Nazis. In fact German troops were often greeted as liberators in the Baltic areas of Latvia, Estonia and Lithuania, and the villages of the Ukraine. A rational regime would have turned this support to its advantage, but the Nazis were not rational. As with Poland, Heinrich Himmler's SS *Einsatzgruppen* (special forces) had followed close behind the front line. Jews and communist officials were murdered as soon as they were found, and the rest of the population were treated with arrogance and cruelty – the Nazis, after all, had indoctrinated their young soldiers to believe that the Slavs were subhuman and fit only for slavery.

The huge size of Russia, and its cruel winters, were major problems for the German army. But in a twist in the tale worthy of a fairy story, the Nazis' evil racist philosophy also proved to be their undoing. Nazi brutality united the Russian people against the invading armies. It gave them the courage and determination to defeat the Germans, in a way their own

▼ Hitler met his match in Soviet dictator Joseph Stalin, a man who was just as cruel and ruthless, but who also made far better use of his military resources.

HEINRICH HIMMLER

The son of a Munich police chief, Himmler had been with Hitler since the days of the Beer Hall Putsch in 1923. As head of Germany's police, including the Gestapo secret police and the SS, he was the man most responsible for carrying out the Nazis' worst atrocities. A gifted and efficient organizer, he blindly obeyed Hitler's every order right until the end of the war, when he tried to negotiate peace with the USA and Britain against Hitler's wishes. This excerpt from a speech he gave to SS generals in 1943 gives a flavour of Nazi attitudes to the people they conquered in the east.

'What happens to a Russian, to a Czech, does not interest me in the slightest...Whether nations live in prosperity or starve to death interests me only in so far as we need them as slaves for our culture...Whether 10,000 Russian females fall down from exhaustion while digging an anti-tank ditch interests me only in so far as the anti-tank ditch for Germany is finished.'

communist masters never could, and led Hitler to complain: 'The Russians fight with a truly stupid fanaticism.' The struggle against the Nazis became known as 'The Great Patriotic War', and it would cost the lives of at least twenty million Soviet citizens.

▲ Heinrich Himmler (above right in uniform) seen with Hermann Göring in 1933 when Himmler was ruthlessly building his power base within Nazi Germany.

COUNTER-ATTACK

By December 1941, the German armies were laying siege to the Soviet Union's two greatest cities, Leningrad and Moscow. But the Soviet armies were now recovering from the initial shock of the invasion and had begun to counter-attack effectively. As the war began to go badly, so Hitler began to fall out with his generals. He failed to concentrate his forces on achieving single objectives, and often changed his own decisions, wasting both valuable time and resources.

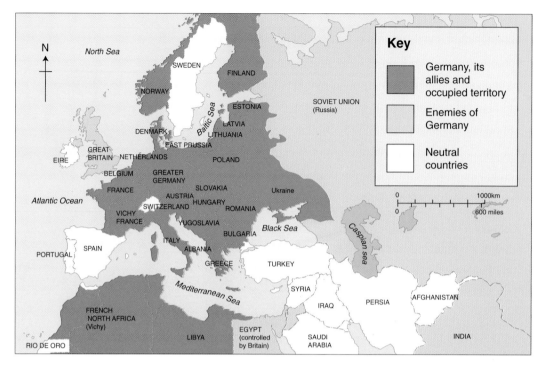

Key

■ Germany, its allies and occupied territory

□ Enemies of Germany

□ Neutral countries

North Sea
SWEDEN
FINLAND
NORWAY
ESTONIA
SOVIET UNION (Russia)
Baltic Sea
LATVIA
DENMARK
LITHUANIA
EAST PRUSSIA
GREAT BRITAIN   NETHERLANDS
EIRE
POLAND
BELGIUM
GREATER GERMANY
FRANCE
SLOVAKIA
Ukraine
AUSTRIA
Atlantic Ocean
SWITZERLAND   HUNGARY
VICHY   ROMANIA
FRANCE
YUGOSLAVIA
Black Sea
BULGARIA
Caspian sea
ITALY
SPAIN   ALBANIA
PORTUGAL
GREECE   TURKEY
Mediterranean Sea
SYRIA
AFGHANISTAN
FRENCH
NORTH AFRICA   IRAQ   PERSIA
(Vichy)
LIBYA   EGYPT   SAUDI   INDIA
RIO DE ORO   (controlled   ARABIA
by Britain)

0   1000km
0   600 miles

▲ This map shows the countries ruled by the German Reich when it was at its greatest extent in 1942.

German soldiers, unprepared for a winter war, suffered terribly in the cold. Soldiers wrapped themselves in tablecloths, or stuffed their boots with straw. Morale sank alarmingly, and the German chief of staff in Russia reported that his troops had reached the end of their tether.

GLOBAL WAR

As the German troops in Russia shivered in their crude shelters and trenches, events in the Pacific island of Hawaii, half-a-world away, were adding to the problems Hitler was creating for his country. In 1936 Germany had made an alliance with Japan. On 7 December 1941, the Japanese launched a surprise attack against the American naval base at Pearl Harbor, Hawaii. Their intention was to destroy America's naval strength and to create a Japanese Pacific empire, much as the Nazis wanted to create their own empire in eastern Europe and Russia.

As Japan's ally, Hitler rashly declared war on the United States too, even though his alliance with Japan did not oblige him to do so. It was a major error. Many Americans

◀ Because Hitler expected the war against Russia to be over in a matter of weeks, ill-equipped German soldiers suffered terribly from lack of warm clothing when winter came.

▼ Soldiers of Germany's ally, Japan, attack Shanghai in their advance through the countries of the Pacific rim. The two allies rarely co-operated effectively during the war.

had wanted their country to keep out of the war against the Nazis – now America suddenly found itself fighting both Japan, who had attacked US forces, and Germany, who had not. For Britain, alone in western Europe in its fight against the Nazis, this was very good news. The United States was the most powerful country in the world. Its population was huge. Its factories, far enough away from both Japan and Germany to be safe from bombing, could produce more aircraft, tanks, ships and guns than any other nation on earth.

As with Italy, Hitler had chosen his allies poorly. Despite Hitler's declaration of war against the USA, the Japanese refused to declare war against Germany's enemy, the Soviet Union. Throughout the war there would be little co-operation between Japan and Germany.

45

HITLER AND STALINGRAD

'There is not a single healthy man left at the front...everyone is at least suffering from frostbite. The commander of the 76th Infantry Division on a visit to the front yesterday came across many soldiers who had frozen to death.'

GERMAN SIXTH ARMY HEADQUARTERS REPORT,
18 JANUARY 1943

'Surrender is out of the question. Troops fight on to the end... Bravery and tenacity of Fortress [meaning Stalingrad] have provided the opportunity to establish a new front and launch counter-attacks. Sixth Army has thus fulfilled its historical contribution in the greatest passage in German history.'

SIGNAL TO SIXTH ARMY FROM HITLER,
22 JANUARY 1943

FURTHER DISASTERS

Hitler had refused to deal with British troops in Africa in 1941. Now this decision came back to haunt him. In 1942 Germany's Afrika Korps were defeated by the British Eighth Army at El Alamein in Egypt. From then on, the southern flank along most of the coast of north Africa would be a secure base from which the USA and Britain could launch attacks against Italy and ultimately Germany.

In a huge struggle in southern Russia, the Germans were defeated in the battle of Stalingrad over the winter of 1942-43. Here Hitler interfered mercilessly in the day-to-day running of the campaign, and seemed to be convinced that his own will and determination could defeat the Russians. Starved of supplies, and caught up in an intense battle fought among the rubble of a ruined city in the depths of winter, the entire German Sixth army was annihilated. Some quarter of a million men were killed or taken prisoner. This was a key turning point in the war. Thereafter, the German army would be pushed slowly but surely all the way back to Berlin in a campaign of terrible brutality.

◄ German soldiers during the battle of Stalingrad in which thousands of their troops were killed. The Soviet victory at Stalingrad marked the turning point of the war against the Nazis.

WAR IN THE AIR

The war was also being brought home to Germany's civilian population. By 1943, US and British bombers were making regular raids over German cities, and thousands of civilians were being killed. Before the war military planners had assumed that bombers would do terrible damage and cause city populations to panic. But, as Hitler too had discovered during the British Blitz of 1940-41, bombing alone did not win wars. Cities and their populations did suffer terribly, but the result was a fierce determination to fight on, rather than panic and surrender.

▲ A US Flying Fortress during a bombing raid over Berlin. British and American bombing of Germany was damaging, but it never caused the all-out destruction Allied commanders hoped that it would.

47

A SECOND FRONT

From 1941 onwards the campaign in the east took up most of Germany's resources. Stalin had been pushing British leader Winston Churchill and US president Franklin Roosevelt to attack Hitler on other fronts too, to take pressure off the Soviet army. Using their African bases, Allied troops landed in Sicily in 1943, and began to advance slowly up through Italy. In the summer of 1943 Mussolini was overthrown and Italy changed sides. Hitler organized a daring commando raid to rescue his friend and the parts of Italy not yet occupied by Allied troops were seized by German soldiers who were stationed there.

Worse still for the Germans was D-Day – a massive invasion of France through Normandy in June 1944. British, Canadian and US troops landed in force. After a hard-fought campaign they reached Paris in August. Germany was now fighting on three fronts and Hitler's dream of a thousand-year Reich was slowly crumbling.

THE FINAL SOLUTION

Hitler termed his vision of a German-dominated Europe a 'New Order'. In his Aryan empire the Jews would no longer exist, and once war broke out the Nazis, under Hitler's orders, began to persecute them with even greater ferocity.

At first, Jews in the conquered eastern territories were deported to ghettos – specific enclosed areas in Polish or Russian cities surrounded by walls and barbed wire. Overcrowded and underfed, many Jews in these ghettos fell victim to diseases such as typhus. But at this stage of the war it was not necessarily the Nazis' intention to exterminate Europe's Jews. There were plans, for example, to deport them en masse to Siberia or the island of Madagascar, but these were abandoned.

The decision to exterminate the Jews seems to have been taken in the summer of 1941. In September of that year SS troops under the command of Reinhard Heydrich were given the job of organizing the 'final solution to the Jewish Question' in Europe. In effect, Heydrich's men were to round up all Jews in Nazi-controlled territory and kill them. Heydrich and SS leader Heinrich Himmler set about organizing this huge task with chilling efficiency. Jews from France to Greece were herded on to freight trains and taken to Poland. The trains were so slow, and the conditions so overcrowded and unhealthy, many of the sick or old died on the journey. When the trains arrived in Poland their passengers were sent to the ghettos or directly to special death camps, such as Treblinka, Belzec, Sobibor and Maidanek. Here millions were killed in specially constructed gas chambers.

Most infamous of all the camps was Auschwitz (survivors of Auschwitz are pictured below on the day they were liberated in January 1945). At least one million Jews were killed there. Arrivals were selected at the railway platform either

for immediate extermination, or to be worked to death in the camp factories. Inmates here, and in other camps, were sometimes subjected to agonizing medical experiments.

In this nightmare world between five and six million Jews were killed, along with other Nazi hate figures, such as gypsies, homosexuals, communists and Jehovah's Witnesses.

CHAPTER EIGHT

1944-1945
The Bitter End

DEFEAT LOOMS

For Hitler's hard-pressed armies, the D-Day Normandy landings were a final, fatal blow. As the massive Soviet army pushed closer to Germany's eastern border, troops were now needed in the west to contain the Allied advance through France. On top of this, British and American soldiers in Italy continued to edge towards Germany's southern border. In Germany itself, Allied bombers pounded factories and cities 24 hours a day. Any sane person could see that Germany had lost the war, yet Hitler was convinced it was still his destiny to win.

German losses in the early victorious campaigns of the war had been slight. Now, as cities burned and army divisions were cut down, the human cost was becoming unbearable. In the heart of Nazi Germany resistance slowly stirred, and discontented army officers began to plot against their *Führer*.

▲ As the French national flag flies from the Arc de Triomphe, German prisoners are paraded in front of press photographers during the liberation of Paris, on 25 August 1944.

VON STAUFFENBERG'S PLOT

'Is there no officer in Hitler's headquarters capable of taking a pistol to the beast?' Colonel Claus von Stauffenberg once confided to a friend. As it happened, Stauffenberg realized that he was just the man for the job. A disabled war hero and chief of staff of the German Home Army (all troops stationed on German soil), he attended briefings with Hitler on a regular basis.

Stauffenberg and other conspirators planned to kill Hitler, and then use Home Army troops to capture key radio and rail stations and to arrest Nazi leaders.

ASSASSINATION ATTEMPT

On 20 July 1944, Stauffenberg flew out from Berlin to a midday conference with Hitler at his headquarters in East Prussia. He carried a bomb in his briefcase, but luck was not with him. The meeting was usually held in an enclosed concrete bunker – a lethal environment for a briefcase bomb. That day it took place in a wooden hut, where the windows were left open because the weather was so hot. Stauffenberg left the bomb as near as he could to Hitler, but seconds before it exploded someone moved the briefcase to the other side of a heavy wooden table leg. It was enough to save Hitler's life. Although four men were killed in the blast, Hitler staggered from the hut alive, his hair singed and his trousers in tatters.

THE PLOTTERS' FATE

Troops loyal to Hitler seized the plotters. Stauffenberg and three other senior conspirators were shot on the spot. They were lucky. Hitler's revenge was terrible. The most senior surviving conspirators were hanged with piano wire – a slow, agonizing death that was filmed for Hitler's benefit, although

CLAUS VON STAUFFENBERG

Handsome, tall and oozing charisma, the aristocratic soldier was said to be the only man in Germany who could stare the *Führer* down. At first he had supported Hitler, but the Nazis' racism, their disastrous conduct of the war, and Stauffenberg's own strong moral code, turned him against them.

Wounded in an air attack in Italy in 1943, he lost an eye, his left hand and two fingers on his right hand. Until the bomb plot, Hitler thought of him as a very glamorous figure. Even the chief SS officer investigating the conspiracy described him as 'a spirit of fire, fascinating and inspiring all who came in touch with him.'

▼ This photograph shows Stauffenberg (left) with Hitler (second right) on one of the colonel's visits to the Nazi leader's East Prussian headquarters.

▶ Hours after Stauffenberg's unsuccessful assassination attempt against him, Hitler shows his ally Mussolini the scene of the bomb explosion.

there is no evidence that he actually watched this. Arrests were made right up to the final days of the war. Altogether, around 3,000 people were executed.

There would be no more assassination attempts. The German army fought grimly on, driven by a combination of fanaticism and backs-to-the-wall desperation. On the eastern front German soldiers knew they could expect little mercy from an enemy they had treated with such cruelty when victory seemed to be theirs.

CRIME AND PUNISHMENT

'I know that he who acts will go down in German history as a traitor; but...if I did not act to stop this senseless killing, I should never be able to face the war's widows and orphans.'

STAUFFENBERG ON HIS DECISION TO TRY TO KILL HITLER

'(This is)...a crime unparalleled in German history. We shall get even with (the traitors) in the way to which we National Socialists are accustomed.'

HITLER ON THE FAILED ASSASSINATION ATTEMPT

GERMANY INVADED

In December 1944, Hitler directed what was to be Germany's last offensive – the so-called 'Battle of the Bulge' in the Ardennes region of France. German troops and tanks were launched in a surprise attack against US and British troops. After some successes the attack ran out of steam, and thereafter Hitler's dreams of victory were confined to his own fevered imagination. He believed that the USA and Britain would fall out with their communist ally, the Soviet Union, and join with him to defeat Stalin. He hoped that new German rockets, the V1 and V2, would visit terrible destruction on Britain.

On the eastern front Soviet troops crossed the German border in January 1945. Thereafter Hitler never left the chancellery and spent most of his final days in an underground bunker headquarters. His health had declined rapidly after the Stauffenberg bomb and he was suffering from nervous exhaustion, bordering on insanity.

GERMANY FACES DEFEAT

Now, instead of the grand dream of a master race ruling over a rich agricultural empire in the east, all that Nazi propaganda could offer the German people was 'Total Victory or Total Ruin'. Hitler ordered that anything of use to the enemy should be destroyed, regardless of the future cost to Germany – bridges, dams, factories, supplies – it was all to go. He told his armament minister Albert Speer 'If the war is to be lost the nation will also perish…The nation has proved itself weak, and the future belongs solely to the stronger eastern nation (Russia). Besides, those who remain after the battle are of little value; for the good have fallen.' Fortunately, this order was largely disobeyed.

HITLER'S LAST DAYS

'He had a special picture of the world, and every fact had to be fitted into that fancied world. As he believed, so the world must be; but, in fact, it was a picture of another world.'

GENERAL HEINZ GUDERIAN

▼ The now unstoppable Soviet army ploughs into East Prussia in January 1945. Here a Red Army tank covered with armed troops is seen in the streets of Mühlhausen.

In one of the most famous photographs of the war, a Russian soldier plants the Soviet flag on top of the Reichstag building in the ruins of Berlin.

THE BATTLE FOR BERLIN

Hitler Youth groups and old men were now sent to fight, and Berlin was defended with a fierce desperation that cost the advancing Soviet army 300,000 casualties. But when Russian gunfire could be heard from Hitler's chancellery bunker, he knew the war was lost. One witness recalls him pacing up and down inside the bunker, raving about the incompetence of his generals, issuing impossible orders to divisions that no longer existed, and waving a map of Berlin around that was slowly disintegrating from the sweat of his hands. The day before he died he dictated his political testament. A bitter, spiteful document, it shows how little Hitler's views of the world had changed – despite the calamity he had brought on Germany.

HITLER'S TESTAMENT

'It is untrue that I, or anyone else in Germany, wanted the war in 1939. It was desired...solely by those international statesmen who were either of Jewish descent or worked for Jewish interests.

...we have lanced the Jewish abscess; and the world of the future will be eternally grateful to us.

...my trust has been misused by many people. Disloyalty and betrayal have undermined resistance throughout the war.'

EXCERPTS FROM HITLER'S POLITICAL TESTAMENT

HITLER'S DEATH

Hitler's friend Mussolini had met a humiliating end. On 28 April 1945, while trying to flee to neutral Switzerland, he and his mistress had been captured and executed by Italian partisans. Their bodies were strung up in a square in Milan to be spat and shot at by embittered Italians.

Hitler was determined to avoid such an undignified exit. On 30 April 1945, with the Soviet troops barely a mile away from the bunker, Hitler and his wife – he had married Eva Braun the previous day – took poison. An aide also shot him through the head to ensure that he was dead. He was 56 years old.

UP IN FLAMES

Their corpses were taken up to the surface and petrol was poured over them. As the bodies were set alight, a heavy Russian bombardment shook the chancellery, and Hitler's entourage stood in the shelter of a porch, giving their *Führer* a final Nazi salute. The charred remains were later given a hasty burial, but the Russians soon uncovered the two corpses. They later had them secretly reburied in asphalt, in a garage in Magdeburg, a city west of Berlin.

Old habits died hard. The German people, whom Hitler had lied to and deceived for twelve years, were told of his death via this grave news announcement: 'This afternoon our *Führer*, Adolf Hitler, at his command post at the Reich Chancellery, fighting Bolshevism to the end, gave his life for Germany.' With solemn music by German composers Wagner and Bruckner playing in the background, the new German head of state, Admiral Dönitz, declared Hitler had died a hero's death, fighting side by side with his soldiers.

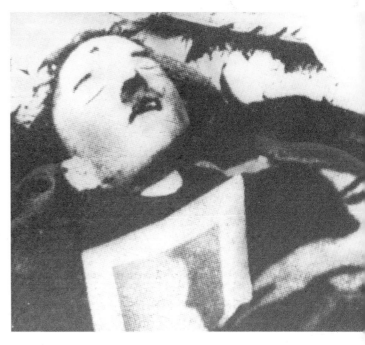

▼ This controversial photograph supposedly shows Hitler after his suicide, just before his body was burned. The picture he is holding is a photograph of his mother, Klara.

CHAPTER NINE

1945-2000
Hitler's Legacy

THE AFTERMATH OF WAR

Stalin spoke for many when he heard the news of Hitler's suicide. 'Now he's done it, the bastard,' he said. 'Too bad he couldn't have been taken alive.' Hitler left Europe in ruins. There are no exact figures for the numbers killed on the continent, but most historians think a figure of around 40 million is broadly accurate. Taking into account this loss of life, and the physical destruction and social upheaval caused by the war, few would disagree with historian D.G. Williamson's description of the Nazi phenomenon as 'a uniquely horrendous event in the history of mankind.'

▼ In an attempt to reveal the full horror of Nazi rule to Germany's population, US soldiers show German civilians the ovens used to burn bodies at Belsen concentration camp.

HITLER'S IMPACT ON HISTORY

> *'By the time he was defeated he had broken down the whole structure of the world in which he lived.'*
>
> ALAN BULLOCK, HISTORIAN AND BIOGRAPHER OF HITLER

SOVIET OCCUPATION

Along with the sheer scale of human misery, there were more long-term consequences for Europe and the world. In trying to build his empire in the east Adolf Hitler paved the way for an eastern empire in the west. Many of the Soviet soldiers who had driven the Nazi armies back to Berlin took ugly revenge on the German population. They raped, looted and killed in vengeance for the terrible brutality visited on their own country by the conquering German army. Then they stayed there. British, French and American troops also occupied the western part of Germany which they had overrun, and set up military bases most of which would remain there for the rest of the century.

Stalin, who over the previous thirty years had twice seen European nations try to crush the Soviet Union, was fearful of another attack. He created 'buffer states' between him and the capitalist nations of western Europe. Generally, with a few exceptions such as Austria, wherever Soviet soldiers had swept away the Nazis, these soldiers remained as occupying forces in those countries. All of eastern Europe was to be ruled by communist states loyal to the Soviet Union for the next forty years. Hitler's Germany was divided into two nations – East and West Germany. An ugly wall divided its former capital Berlin, and minefields and barbed wire divided the country.

▼ In 1946 a released German prisoner of war weeps in the ruins of his home town of Frankfurt.

57

THE COLD WAR

Hitler had long hoped that the Soviet Union would fall out with the United States and Britain, and once the Nazis were crushed, they did. The 'Cold War' that followed the Second World War was a disturbing era of human history, and at times the world seemed on the brink of nuclear war. But that era passed. In 1990 the Soviet regime that had been so strengthened by the defeat of Nazi Germany collapsed. Soviet troops stationed in eastern Europe finally left. The Berlin Wall was pulled down and Germany was reunited.

▲ An East German army guard keeps watch at the Berlin Wall in 1964. The wall became a powerful symbol of the oppressive communist occupation of East Germany during the Cold War.

WHY DID HITLER SUCCEED?

So why was Hitler such a phenomenon? The unique resentment and anger in Germany following defeat in the First World War; Germany's own history of anti-Semitism which allowed Hitler's words to fall on fertile ground; his own talents as a speaker and organizer, and his ability to decisively seize a moment and turn it to his advantage. All these factors combined to raise him to a position of great power, a position from which only a huge global war could remove him.

Hitler's armaments minister, Albert Speer, spoke of the inventive way Hitler, and his propaganda minister Joseph Goebbels made use of new technology: 'Hitler's dictatorship was the first…(to employ) the instruments of modern technology to dominate its own people. By means of such instruments as the radio and public-address system, eighty million persons could be made subject to the will of one individual.'

Hitler's power was unprecedented – no-one before had such an effective combination of unquestioned authority and efficient technology at his disposal. Even Stalin, whose personal power was every bit as great as Hitler's, was hampered by the inefficiencies and vast size of his communist empire.

HITLER AND THE JEWS

In most people's eyes, Hitler's greatest crime was his decision to wipe out the Jews. A whole group of people were singled out to be killed on the basis of an irrational prejudice. Hitler's hatred of the Jews was so great that even when the war was going desperately badly for Germany, resources, manpower and rail transport vital to German armed forces were still diverted to the task of rounding up and killing Europe's Jews. Although there have been other cases of mass-murder and genocide in the world, nowhere else was such an act carried out with such ruthless efficiency.

Britain's wartime prime minister Winston Churchill once described Adolf Hitler as 'a monster of wickedness'. It is difficult to see him in any other way.

HITLER AND THE HOLOCAUST

'Never before had a state...decided that a specific human group, including its aged, its women, its children and its infants, would be killed as quickly as possible and then carried through this regulation using every possible means of state power.'

GERMAN HISTORIAN EBERHARD JÄCKEL, QUOTED IN ALAN BULLOCK'S *HITLER AND STALIN*

▼ Despite leading Germany to total destruction in 1945, the appeal of Hitler and the Nazis still lingers. These pro-Nazi German youths were photographed demonstrating in 1998.

TIMELINE

1889
Hitler born in Braunau, Austria

1903
Hitler's father Alois dies

1907
OCTOBER
Hitler leaves for Vienna
DECEMBER
Hitler's mother Klara dies

1914
AUGUST
First World War begins
Germany is at war with Russia,
France, Britain
Hitler joins the German army
as a regimental messenger

1917
APRIL
USA joins war against Germany
DECEMBER
Russia signs armistice
with Germany

1918
MARCH
Russia surrenders to Germany
at Treaty of Brest-Litovsk
NOVEMBER
First World War ends with
German defeat

1919
JUNE
Treaty of Versailles
SEPTEMBER
Hitler joins German
Workers' Party

1921
Hitler becomes leader of
Nazi Party

1922
Mussolini seizes power in Italy

1923
Nazi's Beer Hall Putsch in
Munich leads to Hitler's arrest.

1924
Hitler sent to jail for
eight months

1925
First volume of *Mein Kampf*
published (second volume
follows in 1926)

1928
Nazi party wins 12 seats at
Reichstag elections

1929
Wall Street Crash brings on
worldwide economic
depression

1930
Nazis win 107 seats in
Reichstag elections

1932
MARCH
Hindenburg defeats Hitler in
German presidential elections
JULY
Nazis win 230 seats in
Reichstag elections

1933
JANUARY
Hitler becomes
German chancellor
FEBRUARY
Reichstag fire
Enabling Act passed – Hitler
becomes dictator of Germany
MARCH
Nazis win 288 seats in
Reichstag elections

1934
JUNE
Night of the Long Knives –
Hitler's rivals within the Nazi
party are eliminated
AUGUST
Hindenburg dies – Hitler
combines role of president and
chancellor, and becomes *Führer*

1935
Nuremberg Laws introduced
depriving Jews of
German citizenship

1936
MARCH
German troops march into the
demilitarized Rhineland
NOVEMBER
Alliance with Japan

1937
Italy joins alliance with
Germany and Japan

1938
MARCH
Seizure of Austria
SEPTEMBER
Munich agreement
Germany occupies Sudetenland
NOVEMBER
Crystal Night — Jewish
synagogues and businesses
attacked throughout Germany

1939
MARCH
Germany occupies rest of
Czech lands
AUGUST
Nazi-Soviet pact
SEPTEMBER
Germany invades Poland
France and Britain declare
war against Germany
Second World War begins

1940
APRIL
Germany conquers Denmark
and Norway
MAY-JUNE
Germany conquers Belgium,
Netherlands and France
AUGUST-SEPTEMBER
Battle of Britain

1941
APRIL
Germany invades Yugoslavia
and Greece
JUNE
Germany invades Soviet Union
DECEMBER
German troops lay siege to
Moscow and Leningrad
Japan at war with USA
following attack on
Pearl Harbor
Hitler declares war on USA

1942
Mass extermination of
Jews begins
SEPTEMBER
Siege of Stalingrad begins
NOVEMBER
German army defeated by
British at El Alamein in Egypt

1943
FEBRUARY
German surrender at Stalingrad
MAY
German and Italian troops
surrender in North Africa
JULY
Mussolini deposed in Italy
AUGUST
German defeat at the Battle of
Kursk marks beginning of the
end of German campaign in
Soviet Union
SEPTEMBER
Allies invade Italy

1944
JUNE
Allies invade France
through Normandy
JULY
Stauffenberg's bomb plot
against Hitler fails
AUGUST
Paris is liberated
DECEMBER
Final German counter-attack in
Ardennes fails

1945
JANUARY
Soviet troops invade Germany
MARCH
Allies cross the Rhine and
invade Germany
APRIL
Mussolini killed by
Italian partisans
Hitler commits suicide with his
wife Eva Braun
MAY
Germany surrenders and the
war in Europe ends
AUGUST
Atomic bombs dropped on
Hiroshima and Nagasaki
Japan surrenders and Second
World War ends

Adulation Intense admiration

Annihilation Total destruction

Anti-semitism Hatred of Jews

Aristocratic From the top level of society

Armament minister Senior government minister in charge of the production of weapons and ammunition

Armistice An agreement between two enemies to stop fighting, and to discuss peace

Armoured vehicle A vehicle which is protected by armour-plating

Artillery Big guns, which fire shells rather than bullets

Atrocities Acts of extreme cruelty, especially murder, usually carried out by soldiers against prisoners of war or civilians

Austro-Hungarian Empire Territory in eastern Europe, which is now made up of Austria, Hungary, the Czech lands, and other Balkan countries

Balkans Area of south-eastern Europe around the Balkan mountains

Blitz, The German bombing campaign against British cities during 1940-1

Bolshevism Alternative name for communism – especially in the Soviet Union

Boycott To refuse to buy goods from

British Commonwealth Countries formerly ruled by Britain, such as Australia, New Zealand and South Africa, which maintain strong ties with Britain

British Empire Countries controlled by Britain as colonies

Buffer state A country which acts as a barrier between two enemy nations

Bunker An underground shelter, usually made of concrete

Chancellery Government headquarters in Berlin

Chief of staff The most senior officer below the commander of an army

Colony A country that is ruled by another country

Commando Soldier trained for hit-and-run raids on an enemy

Communism Political system in which the state controls the wealth and industry of a country on behalf of the people

Communist revolution An event whereby an existing political system is overturned and replaced by a communist system

Concentration camp A prison camp for civilian prisoners – often ruled very brutally

Conspirator Someone who is part of a secret plot

Coup A seizure of power – usually by the military against their own government

Czechoslovakia A country in eastern Europe which is now split into the Czech republic and Slovakia

Demilitarized Referring to territory, and meaning that there are no soldiers there

Democracy Rule of a country by a government elected by the people

Democratic process The business of having an election to decide who should rule a country

Despot An absolute ruler; someone who acts like a tyrant

Dictator A leader who has total, unquestioned control

Diplomatic alliance An agreement between two or more countries, who agree to co-operate with each other

East Prussia Area of north-east Europe, now part of Poland

Economic depression A situation in a country where business and industry is performing badly, there is high unemployment, and money is losing its value

Entourage A group of people who accompany an important person

Extremist Some one who behaves in a fanatical, unreasonable way to put forward their political ideas

Fanaticism Blind, aggressive devotion to a political idea

Fascist party Broadly speaking, any political party which is very right wing, having one unquestioned leader, and pursuing extremist policies

Flank A military term meaning the left or right side of a manoeuvring army formation

Freight train A train designed to carry goods, rather people

Führer A German word meaning leader

Genocide The deliberate destruction of an entire race of people

Germanic From Germany, or part of German culture

Germanic stock People from Germany or of German ancestry

Ghetto An area of a city or town where a particular group of people are forced to live

Gutter press Particular type of newspaper which reports sensationalist stories, often with no regard to actual events or accuracy

Ideology A political idea or philosophy

Illegitimate Referring to a child born to an unmarried couple

Indoctrination The uncritical teaching of one political idea

Inflation Economic situation where the value of money goes down, and prices for goods and property go up

Lance-corporal A rank in the army, just above that of private

Lay siege A military term meaning to surround an enemy in a city or fortified place and attempt to force them to submit

Liberator Someone who frees people from an oppressive regime

Mein Kampf A book written by Hitler outlining his political ideas

Minister of the interior Government officer in charge of the way the country is controlled – especially the police

Motorized infantry Soldiers who are moved around in lorries or other forms of transport
Munitions Ammunition for guns and artillery

Nationalist Someone who is an uncritical supporter of his own country – right or wrong

Occupying force An army that has taken over another country

Pageant Colourful parade or ceremony
Partisans Soldiers who carry on fighting an enemy, even though their country has been conquered
Persecution Persistent and aggressive oppression of a person or group of people
Phenomenon An unusual event
Political agenda A series of policies that are characteristic of a particular political philosophy
Political agent A spy sent to spy on a political party
Political fanatic Somebody whose devotion to a political idea is unthinking and aggressive
Political philosophy The beliefs of one kind of political party
Political rallies Gatherings held to put over the views of a political party
Political testament A series of opinions and wishes set out by a politician who is giving up power
Prejudice An unthinking dislike of people of another race, culture or country
Propaganda Biased information which puts forward the views of a government or political party in order to persuade people to think in a particular way
Propaganda newsreel A film, shown in cinemas, containing propaganda

Racial resettlement The removal and resettlement of a group of people of one specific race
Referendum Vote by the people of a country on one specific issue

Salvation To be saved from harm or imprisonment
Scapegoats A group of people unfairly blamed for a disaster or misfortune
Self-propelled artillery Artillery which can move under its own power, rather than artillery which has to be towed by another vehicle
Slavs A racial group concentrated in eastern Europe and Russia
Social upheaval Disturbance in a country which affects the civilian population
Socialist A supporter of socialism – a milder form of communism
Soviet Union Area of eastern Europe and Russia established in 1922 and controlled by the communist party based in Moscow. Now split into Russia and many other independent states
Sterilization A medical term meaning to make it impossible for a man or woman to have children
Supply line System of transport whereby an army is kept supplied with food and weapons

Trajectory The path that a flying object takes through the air
Treason The act of rebellion against one's own government and country
Treaty An agreement made between two or more countries
Trench warfare A type of fighting common during the First World War, in which opposing armies in trenches faced each other across an area of 'no-man's land'
Typhus An often fatal disease causing fever and skin rashes

Western Front Battleground during the First World War in north-west Europe where British, French and German soldiers fought each other

Yugoslavia Country in eastern Europe now made up of Bosnia, Croatia and other smaller nations

FURTHER INFORMATION

BOOKS
Adolf Hitler (Heinemann Profiles)
Adolf Hitler (Heinemann Leading Lives, 2001)
Two good books for KS2 and KS3/4 respectively.

Hitler – A Study in Tyranny
by Alan Bullock (Pelican 1975)
Originally published in 1952, and still considered to be the best general account of Hitler's life.

Hitler and Stalin – Parallel Lives
by Alan Bullock (Fontana Press 1993)
Bullock builds on his original biography of Hitler to give an updated, compelling account of the dictator's life.

The Third Reich by D.G. Williamson (Longman 1998)
Dry but rigorous account of Hitler and the Nazi era.

Inside the Third Reich
by Albert Speer
(Weidenfeld & Nicolson 1970)
Fascinating insight by one of Hitler's closest lieutenants.

A Social History of the Third Reich
by Richard Grunberger
(Penguin 1974)
Riveting account of day-to-day life inside Hitler's Germany

WEBSITES
A search on the Internet revealed some half a million Hitler-related websites. Please treat them cautiously, as many sites have been set up by pro-Nazi groups. The following offer useful information for further research:
http://www.encyclopedia.com/ articles/05933.html
A good potted introduction

http://www.bbc.co.uk/ education/modern/hitler/ hitlehtm.htm
A reliable and thorough resource

INDEX

WARWICK
LIBRARY
SCHOOL